HIGHSCHOOL SWEET HEARTS!

Rebekah Mitchell-Wagner

For my friends who attended and still attend East Davidson High School.

Table of contents

- ❖ Chapter 1
  - ➢ Freshman Year
- ❖ Chapter 2
  - ➢ Sophomore Year
- ❖ Chapter 3
  - ➢ Junior Year
- ❖ Chapter 4
  - ➢ Senior Year
- ❖ Chapter 5
  - ➢ College Life

Freshman Year!

You will find in life that love is not perfect. Love can be something great but it can also hurt like a bitch all at the same time, it can cut you so deep that you just want to crawl in a hole and die and not try again. Most of the time though true love is worth the pain, not all times, but most times. In the case of my first love it wasn't worth the pain but it taught me valuable lessons.

It was my first week as a freshman at East Davidson High School in Thomasville, North Carolina. It started out okay, I met a lot of new people and I liked most of my classes. I didn't really feel scared about starting high school because I had my cousin Marie to talk to if I needed her. Marie was cool somewhat, she was a junior with red hair and she was short like me. The only bad thing about my cousin is she had a reputation of sleeping around at East.

My week started out great until that third day of school when I laid eyes on him and my heart stopped. By him I mean Billy Everett. Billy Everett wasn't the typical jock at East but he was popular.

He stood about five foot four inches tall with tan skin and big strong muscles. His hair was straight and brown and his eyes were a dark sexy brown. He was very attractive, all the girls liked him and wanted him and the sad part was almost all the girls at East Davidson High School had him at least once, he was what you would call a man hoe. He loved sex but was afraid of commitment.

Billy and my friends Leigh and Tony and I all had lunch together that first semester and each day at lunch I would sit with them and occasionally talk to Billy. Our conversations would always start out random but that was just Billy. Our conversations would range from things like class, the military and anime cartoons. Every time I talked to him I wanted to know more and more about him.

It was toward the middle of September and all I could do was think about Billy and I couldn't figure out why. I had an amazing boyfriend named Roy so why could I not get this guy out of my head? I wondered what I should do. One morning I asked Marie what I should do because she knew him a little too well. I mean she had dated him once.

"Beka just try to forget about him, yes he may look sexy but he is a man hoe and an ass to girls. Trust me, I know I dated him and truthfully he would probably never go for a girl like you. You are fourteen and he is seventeen so just forget it."

I knew she was probably right but I still gave him my number after fourth period that day anyway, I secretly wanted her to be wrong and for some reason I liked him more than Roy I guess it was because I hardly ever got to see Roy and I got to see Billy every day.

    Later that night about six o'clock my phone rung, I was doing math homework so I debated on answering it for a few seconds, finally I decided sure why not. I was in shock when I did because it was Billy. He had just gotten off of work, which at that time was working as a landscaper. We talked for a few minutes then I sadly went back to my algebra homework.

Which sucked because math was one of my worst subjects.

After that night Billy and I became good friends and we would talk at lunch and on the phone sometimes at night. We just didn't let his normal friends know because I was not what you would say popular. His friends consisted of Ian Johnson- A tall skinny basketball player, Tony Stevens- The average guy that sits with us at lunch, Katie Goings- A Stuck up sophomore that loved Billy and Smink Bowers- The nerdy kid who actually was not that bad. Smink was actually cool just like Tony except unlike Tony, Smink didn't have a secret crush on me.

A couple days later at lunch Leigh, Tony, Billy and I were sitting outside at the picnic tables when I asked Billy

"How is your day going so far?"

"Boring as ever, how is yours?"

"Sucky, I hate my math class." I responded.

Billy then went to another table that had a bunch of girls sitting at it and started to flirt and talk about partying. He could never stay on one topic and he was such a big flirt. That is who he was but I didn't mind. I was day dreaming about Billy when Leigh sat down beside me.

"Beka, Tony is so cute and I want to talk to him I just don't know how."

"Girl I have known you since sixth grade and you have never been shy before. Just go talk to him like you would any other guy."

For once she took my advice and soon after those two became an item even though they only lasted a couple months because they were too much alike.

Months passed and the semester was almost over. It was December a couple nights before Christmas and Billy called me and asked to come over to my house to hang out. My mom said sure because she was ready to meet the boy that she heard me talk about all the time and she couldn't stand Roy. We had to get a few things at Wal-Mart so Billy decided to meet us there so he could follow us back to my house.

Right off the bat my mom liked him. She liked his good looks and his charming personality, she even insisted that I dump Roy for him. Once we got back to my house we hung out for a bit, laughed about crazy stuff, and talked about everything under the sun he even found my tickle spot and rolled me off the couch. I am still lucky I didn't end up with a bruise from that.

When it was time for him to leave he looked at me like he was waiting for me to escort him out, but my dummy self-sat on the couch and watched him leave. Later that night he called me,

"Hey I was wanting you to follow me outside." I smiled to myself and asked

"Why?"

"I was going to kiss you that's why, but oh well you didn't come outside."

"I'm sorry, I'm not very good with hints."

"Yeah I can see that." he said.

When we hung up my head was spinning and my heart was jumping in loops. I didn't know what to think or do because we both were taken and I was actually friends with Shell (His girlfriend at the time). At that moment though I just wanted to slap myself in the face. I knew I was with Roy but I really wanted that kiss and I was determined to get it.

    A couple days went by and he came over to my house again. School was out for Christmas break and New Year's so it was the perfect time for him and I to sneak around. We watched movies and this time chilled in my bedroom with the door open. All along while we watched the movie sitting so close together I longed so bad for his touch. I wanted to feel the touch of his lips all over my body and as I sighed at the thought of it, it was like he could sense it because he smiled. When he left I made sure to follow him out.

He pushed me up against his truck and kissed me passionately. It was better than I had imagined and it was so passionately that it sent shivers down my spine and it sent me to cloud nine all at the same time. I knew right then and there that I was in love with him.

We kissed for what seemed like ever but I didn't mind. I just wanted to cherish the moment. The only disadvantage was he was a little taller than I, but his blue Nissan did a good job at helping. After the kiss I went back in and I heard my mom say,

"Miss Mitchell you have a boyfriend remember that and even though I despise his guts that was wrong out of you. If you are going to smooch on that boy at least break up with the one you got first."

I nodded then went to my room and started banging my head against my wall because that's what I do when I get into sticky situations. It's painful and I always have a headache after wards but it helps.

A week went by and school went back in. It was January a whole new year. On January 5th it was my birthday and I was finally fifteen and I was having a party. I was a little nervous because Billy would be coming and so would Roy. Billy knew about Roy, but Roy didn't know about the sneaking around with Billy so I didn't know what would happen. I hadn't really hung out with Billy much since the kiss so I was excited to being seeing him outside of school.

When two finally rolled around I was having a very good time. I got a Scooby Doo balloon from my momma and Roy had gotten me a necklace for my birthday and I loved it but I felt bad for sneaking around behind his back. I didn't get to see him very much even though he was eighteen because he lived in Roxboro which is close to Raleigh and he didn't have his licenses.

A couple of hours passed and Billy finally showed up and when he did he gave me a big bear hug which made Roy a little jealous. Shortly after Billy arrived Roy left and when he did mom and my nanny took full advantage of it.

They pushed me down on Billy's lap and started taking pictures. My nanny like momma hated Roy but loved Billy. They didn't like Roy because to them he always acted like a know it all. After the party I got an after party make out session from Billy and loved every minute of it. I thought it was the best birthday present ever.

January went by rather quickly and we were still sneaking around outside of school and everyone caught on. Everyone would smirk when they saw us except for Shell of course. All of the sneaking around made me love him and want him that much more and I was determined to make him mine. Exams were in a couple days and Billy had offered me a ride home on the 4th period exam day and I said I would talk to mom.

On the week of the exams I passed the first three and I was excited about the fourth period one because Billy would be taking me home. After the exam I met up with him with my heart pounding and quickly jumped in his truck and we were off. When we got to my house he kissed me furiously and I looked at him and nodded. Then thinking that it wouldn't look suspicious I left the front door open after we went into the house.

We went to my bedroom quickly and I found myself removing my shirt and his and kissing him roughly. I felt his hands move along my body and my heart began to beat faster because this was what I wanted. I had just got his pants undone when I heard,

"Bea Dawn" first thing that went through my head was damn! Then I heard,

"You have two seconds to get out here or I am coming in there."

I quickly looked at Billy, jumped up and grabbed my shirt. I then raced in there and saw my nanny standing in the kitchen with her arms propped up on her hips.

"Just what were you two doing in there?" I am a horrible liar but I said the first thing that came to my mind.

"Looking for Sassy, I couldn't find her."

"And that requires you getting off the bed?"

"She was stuck between the box and the desk and Billy got her out I was sitting there."

Just to be clear nanny didn't buy any of this, she knew I was lying threw my teeth and Sassy was my dog that I just got, she was six weeks old at the time.

After that Billy left and nanny called momma at work and told her that she caught Billy and me trying to have sex. Mom said we would discuss it when she got home and Billy came back over and we did. She was not mad but not very happy about it either.

She told us never to do it in the house again and we didn't. After the POW WOW I guess you could call it I walked out with Billy.

"Trying to find Sassy huh?"

"Well you came up with a whole bunch of nothing. I said the first thing that came to my brain."

"Next time think of something better."

"I'll try but I'm not making any promises." I said smiling. He kissed me then left.

Billy and I still had lunch together that second semester. Tony and Leigh didn't have it with us instead Marie and my other friend Nicole did. A couple weeks later after getting caught, I finally got the courage to tell Roy the truth about Billy.

I was tired of all the sneaking around, I was starting to feel like a slut and I didn't like it. Billy had even broken up with Shell that day and he was finally available so I thought just maybe things would start to change but boy was I wrong. He had another girlfriend the next day.

More weeks went by and Billy and I became distant and Roy and I got back together even though I knew it was wrong. Everything felt normal again, Roy and I started hanging out again on the weekends. I studied more in my classes and I sat by myself at lunch and did homework. This lasted for about a month then Billy one day approached me again at lunch.

"Hey why have you been so distant from me lately?"

"Billy I love you, and I can't stand just being friends anymore."

"I have a girlfriend Beka."

"I know but I'm so tired of sneaking around, you either want me or you don't." I told him.

"Hey can I come by later so we talk about this?" "I guess" I said as the bell rung to end lunch.

He came by later that evening and the sneaking around started again it was as if nothing had changed. It was like I was his play toy. My cousin caught on very quickly because one we would act funny around one another at school and two because she would catch glimpses of the red marks on my neck. But little did she know that we had almost made it to third base.

Now Marie if she wanted to could be a royal bitch, which is what she turned into when she realized that Billy and I were sneaking around again. She hated that Billy was into me, She hated it so much that she would do just about anything to keep us apart and keep things stirred between us. She would even have random girls come up to him and make out with him in front of me and Billy wouldn't care, actually he enjoyed it. One of those girls was even Nicole.

It was April 20th and I was having a great day until lunch. Marie was still trying to come in between Billy and me and that day it worked. She had Nicole make out passionately with Billy in front of me and it offended me and hurt me at the same time. I walked the other direction crushed because I truly did love him. Marie on the other hand was smiling from ear to ear as I walked. After that I was determined to never speak to either of the three again. No matter how bad it would rip me apart to never speak to Billy again.

Later that night at home I wrote Billy a message on Myspace telling him to have a happy life and to act like I never existed because I couldn't take being without him any longer and that he could take Marie and Nicole and shove them right up his ass. I also told him that I was tired of being his play toy and to never call me again.

I then broke up with Roy for the last time so that I could clear my head and figure out what I wanted. When Billy received the message, he kept ringing my phone and leaving messages, so finally I put the song " Not Ready to Make Nice" by the Dixie Chicks on my answering machine because it described how I was feeling. After that he finally quit calling.

All day the next day it was really hard ignoring him especially in the halls. After first period he tried to grab my shoulders it wasn't easy getting away but I did. Then third period came around and I was the last one out of Earth Science because one of my boot buckles came undone. As I looked back up he was there standing over me. He begged me to talk to him so I turned to walk the long way to lunch; he quickly caught up and grabbed me by the arm almost knocking me off balance.

"Beka please talk to me." He begged.

"I don't want to talk, let me go." I said,

He let me go but then looked me deep in the eyes and after that I couldn't move. My heart began to thump loudly. He then said,

"When is the next time that you are going to be single?" I responded with a smile on my face,

"I already am."

"Well, now you are not."

As he said that he darted up the stairs. I caught up to him while thinking what a corny way of asking someone out. He then kissed me passionately and we went on to lunch side by side.

When we got to the cafeteria, I walked in by myself because he had to go talk to the army sergeant since in two short months after graduation he would be going to basic training for the army reserves. After getting in the cafeteria I told Nicole the good news and went and got my lunch. When I sat down beside him at our table since we decided to sit inside this semester, Marie started cussing at me and saying,

"You said you were never going to date her."

She then got up and stormed off.

A lot of people were mad when they found out Billy and I had gotten together including his friend Katie, but they got over it. I had finally gotten what I had wanted and I was determined not to let anyone mess it up. Billy was mine and I wanted it to stay that way no matter what. Later that evening when I got home I told my mom the good news and she was happy. Her response was

"Well it's about time."

On Friday night a week later we wanted to hang out, so my mom, brother and I had to go get him because a couple days right after we had gotten together he wrecked his truck, well more like rear ended his boss by accident. I was happy but nervous at the same time because it was time to meet his mom.

Angel was really cool, I thought, but I was worried that she didn't like me. We left his house and went and hung out with my mom's friend James who she had known since she was a kid. James and Billy hit it off really well, which didn't surprise me because everyone loved Billy.

"So how did you like James?" I asked when it was time to go.

He was cool." Billy said while wrapping his arms around me.

At that moment I felt so snug and warm that all I wanted was to stay right there forever. When it was time to take him home he softly whispered in my ear, "I love you!" My heart, after hearing those words, leaped with so much joy that I couldn't stand it, I wanted to be his forever. I went home that night happy as a lark.

That Sunday Billy got to drive his mom's car so he, my brother and I all went to church together. As soon as we got there he introduced me to everyone and then disappeared. As I turned and looked around he came around the corner with two little boys, one on his back and the other around his neck. He was great with kids and when I told him that he looked at me and said,

"Well, I'll be better with ours."

I simply smiled at the thought and followed him through the hall.

His church was amazing and he helped gather the offering and things like that. He was a good Christian boy. At the end of the service the pastor announced that in June which was two months away that Billy would be going to basic training. I was proud of Billy because he was going to be going to learn how to defend our country and he was going to be my soldier.

After that day was when things started to go downhill. I called him the next day after school to see if we were still going to hang out, and he was at Katie's house. I didn't know what to think, I wanted to trust that he would never cheat on me so I let it slide but it still bugged me.

The next week was a good week. I saw Billy after school a lot but that weekend he had drill so I didn't get to see him that was okay because that Monday was his 18th birthday which was May 4th. So while he was at drill I went to my pappy to get him a birthday present.

Pappy had a collection of pocket knives and I thought that would be the best thing to give him. I made sure he came over to my house after school on his birthday.

"Babe, you didn't have to get me anything."

"I know, but I wanted to."

I said while handing him the knife that had a turkey on it. He didn't stay long because he was still tired from drill over the weekend but he did get his present and a birthday kiss so I was happy.

    The next day at school was a horrible one for me because someone decided to start a horrible rumor that I was sleeping with my chorus teacher. Still to this day I don't know who started it and still to this day the chorus teacher hates me because that was his job on the line and it was a week before his wedding when the rumor got started.

I spent most of that morning in Mrs. Smith, the principal's office trying to get it worked out. She knew it wasn't true and that I didn't start it but we still had to discuss it because that was her job. After getting out of her office I just wanted to crawl into Billy's arms and cry my eyes out.

"Baby its okay, how about I come over after school later? Will that cheer you up?"

I smiled and nodded and went back to class even though I was angry.

Later that evening Billy kept his word and came over. He looked so handsome, he was dressed in blue jeans and a brown Abercrombie tee shirt and he smelled so good. I walked right up to him, wrapped my arms around his neck, and kissed him softly. We didn't want to stay inside because it felt perfect outside so we stretched out on the steps and looked at the stars for a while. To me it was romantic. Then he asked me,

"Did Roy and you not do this kind of stuff?"

"No because we really never got to see each other that much."

I said while lying in his arms. I wanted to fall asleep, but I knew I couldn't because he had to leave soon even though he said I could.

The next day at school Billy was in a rather good mood, when I got to school I walked out into the Eagle Court. The Eagle Court was a court yard area with a big eagle statue in the middle of it. That's where most of my friends or "The Group" as we were called hung out at during the day. When I walked up to Billy that morning he was talking to Smink, Marie, Katie, Cassie, Meredith, Leigh,

Tony and Nicole. Ian had not arrived yet.

Cassie was my other buddy who wore glasses and liked rock music. She was in chorus class with me along with Leigh and Nicole. As I was talking with Cassie I felt a hand grab my waist and toss me up and before I knew it I was being tossed around like a sack of potatoes in the air. Billy knew I was afraid of heights so I was too scared to scream.

When he finally sat me down I was furious and he was laughing so hard his face was red. I had never wanted to slap him so bad in my life.

"Oh come on babe it was not that bad." I just glared at him and gave him the finger and went to class.

When lunch came around he asked,

"Are you still mad at me?"

"No I guess not" I then leaned down to give him a kiss.

"Nope you avoided me all day now you're going to have to wait."

"Oh you ass that is not fair."

He then laughed told me he loved me and went to talk to another friend at another table. Before the bell rung he asked me if I wanted to ride to Lexington with him and Ian after school to look at Yugioh cards. I told him sure that I would text mom during fourth period and that I would meet him out front after school.

 After meeting up out front I found Billy and kissed him and found that Ian was in the front seat. I looked at Billy and Billy's response was

"Hey that's Ian's spot sorry."

I didn't feel like arguing so I just got in the back and dealt with it. When we arrived at the card shop I found some that I thought were cool because Yugioh was another thing that Billy and I had in common. I had quite the collection of cards myself. After they purchased a few cards he dropped me off at my house and kissed me bye.

The next few weeks went by really fast and the next thing I knew it was June and I only had a few more weeks with him until he would be gone to basic training for two months. It was the night before Senior Awards Day and Billy called.

"Hey babe do you want to leave early with me tomorrow?"

"Yes I would love to, but can I? I am not a senior?"

"Yes as long as your mom writes you a note."

"Okay well I will see you tomorrow I'm going to bed good night love you."

"Love you too and babe wear something easy to get off."

That morning when I got up I dressed extra special for Billy I knew what he had in mind and so did momma but she didn't say anything. When I got to school I didn't get to see Billy that morning because he had to go down to the gym and when it was time for the underclassmen to go down I put my note in the box and sat down. After the three hour assembly was finally over I quickly went and found him waiting on me in the car.

"It's about time you got here."

"I had to get away from the globs of people." I said as I got in.

We then went to his house because he claimed he had to pick something up but I knew what was going on. When we got to his house he hurried out and I slowly unbuckled my seat belt and hurried up the steps after him. As I was walking in he was coming out of his room with something in his hands.

He walked up to me and slowly kissed me while lying me down on the floor. The touch of his hands made my heart pound heavily but I liked it. As he lifted up my shirt he kissed me softly and all I could think about was this was the moment that I had been waiting for. Until he stopped right in the middle when we had just got started good and said

"Let's go eat I am hungry".

Talk about angry I was downright furious.

We left his house after about thirty minutes and went to the best Chinese restaurant ever China Garden

Buffet. We each got our food to go because it was jammed packed with East Davidson students.

We went back to my house and ate and after he ate he had to go because he had to go get something from a lady that went to his church. I kissed him softly and waved bye and when he left I went and put my things from school in my bedroom. From that moment I knew for a fact that he loved me, I was sure of it.

When my mom got home she yelled that she wanted me in her room, so I went to see what she wanted.

"Did you two use protection?" She asked me.

I was shocked because I hadn't told her anything

"Yes momma"

"Was it good?"

"Yes"

"Okay making sure"

After her saying that I kind of just wanted to faint but she was laughing about it. If it would have been with any other guy she would have not been like that. I then told her about what he done to me because we have a good relationship like that and she started busting out laughing and nodding her head at the same time. I told her it was not funny at least it wasn't to me.

Billy called later and I felt so happy to hear his voice. I told him that I dreaded the week from the coming up Monday because he would be leaving and that I didn't know what I was going to do all summer. I knew one thing for certain, I would wait on him and stay faithful which I did. We talked about how I wished he would be able to call me and he didn't know if he would be able to or not but he would try.

I woke up the next morning dreading school because the final exams started the next day and I knew the teachers would be pounding their students with review work and lectures. I got to school and walked into the Eagle Court and Billy was already there

"Good morning beautiful" Billy said while wrapping his arms around me.

"Morning darling, I want to go back to bed. I didn't sleep very well last night, Bad dreams again." I said while yawning.

Everything was going peachy that morning, even Katie was being nice, that was until Ian walked outside.

"So Beka, I heard that you and Billy had fun yesterday."

Ian said while laughing. I looked around and said unhappily

"You told Ian! Who else did you tell?"

I was really angry that all I wanted to do was punch him because personal things like that were supposed to remain personal.

"Babe, it's not like he is going to tell anybody." I wanted to cuss him so bad but he was saved by the bell for first period. I responded with a sigh and said

"Okay"

I then kissed him and went to class. I walked to first period still really angry. When I got to class I sat down beside my other cousin Lyndsay and Nicole. Nicole like chorus had first period with me which was parenting.

"I heard about yesterday, how was it?"

Nicole said smiling. I was so mad but I only let my blushing show.

"Who else knows about this?"

I asked Nicole kind of loudly.

"What, what is going on? My cousin asked,

Before I could say, "Never mind,"Nicole had already blurted it out.

"Yuck Beka, you had sex with him? That is gross."

I didn't want to get loud so I simply buried my head in my arms.

After first period I went to find Billy and when I did I softly punched him.

"Wasn't going to tell anybody huh!"

"Babe calm down, what is everyone saying?"

The whole school knew by now even people I didn't know.

"Oh, nothing just that I am pregnant and asking questions!!"

I was so angry so I was talking louder than I thought.

"Okay, babe, I will take care of it I promise, I love you."

I told him I loved him too and walked to English by myself, which wasn't normal. I had English honors with Mrs. Janice the class was okay but I loved her as a teacher. This was the class where I could actually think and get away from everything. The best part was no one really aggravated me either.

"Hey baby, how was second?"

Billy asked while waiting for me outside the door.

"Not long enough" I said while taking a sigh.

"Try not to worry about it too much, I took care of it."

That was the best thing I heard from him all day, but I didn't know how long the peace was going to last. He walked me to third period like normal and kissed me softly. I walked into Earth Science thinking about how much I loved him.

"So Beka, what sex is the baby?"

I heard one of the trouble makers say. I just simply rolled my eyes and sat down. I didn't have any friends in that class since that class was really nothing but trouble makers. That class had been the worst all day and all I wanted to do was cry but I didn't, even though they still continued to pick on me and say mean jokes throughout the class period. I didn't stoop to their level instead I continued to do my review packet and mind my own business.

I was so excited when the bell rung that I ran out and waited on Billy.

"Baby, what is wrong? You look like you are about to cry?"

"Trust me, I want to right now." I whispered when he found me.

He got mad when I wouldn't tell him what was wrong, so he softly pushed me against the wall and asked,

"Beka what is wrong?"

"Everyone keeps saying that I am pregnant, and cracking jokes and being mean. Baby I don't know what to do." I said with a sigh.

"Beka, just ignore them, people are not worth it and you're not pregnant." he said while kissing me.

After that the day went great. When I got home I sat down and did my exam review with a clear mind. When my mom got home she, my brother and I went out to eat at a little restaurant named Sunrise Diner. I was happy because I needed some country cooking to take the rest of the stress away.

After supper we went home and Billy called me he told me he had finally just gotten home from PT, he couldn't talk long because it was rough and he was tired. Then I guess what everyone were saying got to me because I asked him,

"Billy, what are we going to do if I am pregnant?"

"Beka you're not, but even if you were it would be okay."

I smiled to myself and said "I love you"

We got off the phone and I went to bed hoping tomorrow would be better.

 I woke up the next morning and realized that it was Friday and it was the day for first period exams and I hadn't even studied. I got to school, kissed Billy and wished him good luck on his exam. He had to take his in the cafeteria since he was a senior so I walked to parenting alone again.

 "Hey, Beka are you ready for the EOC?" Nicole asked.

"No not really. To be honest I had forgotten it was today." I said as I sat down in my seat.

Come to find out that exam was easy and I passed it with a seventy-five.

After the exam I went and found Billy. He had passed his exam too. The rest of my exams the next couple days went by smooth and I passed every single one of them. On the last day of school after the last exam Billy and I had decided that we were going to go get a pregnancy test to prove to everyone that I wasn't pregnant.

When the bell finally rung Nicole and I walked out of chorus together. I quickly found Billy and walked with him to the car. We had to hurry because we were picking up Ian then we were going to Wal-Mart. I was mad that he had told Ian about what we were getting, so I stayed in the front seat just to piss him off.

"I told her to get in the back, man." Billy said when we got to Ian's.

At that moment I had felt like slapping them both. My mom was getting off work early that day so she was texting me. I told her what was going on and she went off. We had gotten the test and was in Taco Bell getting lunch when she called me.

"Why is he getting you a test? You are not pregnant, you just got off your period!" She was screaming at me so I went outside and got back into the car with Ian.

Billy had gotten us cheesy beef burritos, which were delicious. He dropped me off at home and as I got out of the car he stopped me and told me,

"I will call you later, but whatever happens I love you and everything will be okay."

I smiled and kissed him. When my mom got home, I took the test and, thank goodness it was negative because I wasn't ready to be a mom. I wanted to have kids someday just not yet.

"See I told you so," my mom said.

I quickly called Billy and told him. After getting off the phone with him I laid down thinking the scare is over.

    I had dreaded that Monday coming up because he was leaving for basic and I hated it because I wouldn't be seeing him for two months. Friday came which meant Monday inched closer and I had only seen Billy once since the last day of school because he had been so busy packing but he was having a going away party the next day and I was hoping he would want me to come so I could be with him one last time before he left.

    Later that night he called me when he got time

"Hey baby, do you want me to come and get you tomorrow?"

"Of course, you don't even have to ask."

I told him that I would most likely by at nanny's because she and momma had finally gotten the pool set up. He said he would pick me up around two the next day. After that it was late so I went to bed.

When I woke up the next morning I got up, ate breakfast, got dressed and off to nanny's we went. I watched momma, my brother and nanny play in the pool. I walked around outside and played with Copper and the cats as I waited. I would have chilled with pappy for a little bit too but he was already out on his Saturday morning stroll when we got there.

When it was finally about two Billy called me and asked me if I was ready because he had to go pick Tony up also. When he arrived at nanny's he had already gotten Ian so, of course, I had to get in the back. When my nanny noticed she piped up and yelled,

"Billy, why is your friend in the front and my granddaughter in the back?"

I busted out laughing and smiled. Billy's smile faded and for a while everything stayed quiet. After we picked up Tony he also had something to say about Ian being the front.

"Billy why on earth is Beka in the back and Ian in the front? That is very rude man."

I looked at Tony and responded,

"I'm used to it Tony its okay."

When we got to Billy's house I met most of his family and they all seemed really nice. His cousin Tiffany and I hit it off really well. I also helped some of the guys set up some things like some of the chairs and picnic tables and I hoped that maybe sometime before I left I would get to have some alone time with Billy.

Shortly after the party started Billy started acting like I wasn't even there. Every time I would walk over to be with him he would suddenly have something to do. So I started to feel really hurt and bothered.

"Beka what is the matter with you? You're not smiling today like normal." Tony asked me.

"It's nothing Tony, please don't worry about it."

"Beka you can talk to me, you know that."

I smiled and told him how Billy had been acting since we had arrived and how lately he had been acting really distant from me.

"Beka, I'm so sorry that he is treating you like this and frankly I think it is crap. You are supposed to be the most important thing to him."

"Thanks Tony but I really don't feel like I am. Do you think you can talk to him for me?" I asked softly.

"Yeah sure, but Beka, you do know that if you were with me that I would never treat you like this." Tony had said before walking away.

I didn't like Tony like that so him saying that made me feel a little awkward.

    After the party I was helping Billy's mom clean up when I noticed Tony coming out of the house. He looked at me and said,

"I talked to him but I don't know how much good it done."

I told him thanks and went to take the hot dog buns and the mayonnaise in the house. As I was sitting the stuff down on the table, I noticed Billy was putting things up in the fridge when I heard him slam something down. I then looked up to find him running out the door and Ian and Tony beside me. I gave Tony a glance like what did you say to him before going to look for Billy. I went looking for him in the woods because that was his number one place he liked to go but he wasn't there instead it was all trees.

When I got back to the house I found Billy in the kitchen looking at me with sad eyes and that broke my heart even more. I asked him if I could talk to him alone so we went outside on his front porch and I started to tell him how I felt. I knew it wasn't sinking in because right when I was about done his cousin showed up and he got up right when I was in the middle of my sentence and walked around the house.

I met his cousin and actually liked him. After Billy and he talked, I took Billy back around to the front and tried talking to him again, but it still didn't work. So after I was done I sat down and sighed and looked up to find Billy standing over me. He leaned down and kissed me so passionately that it made my head spin and I thought, was he actually listening?

Billy and I walked back around the house and I looked over and smiled at Tony. Then Billy asked the boys and me,

"I'm going to Wal-Mart to get some more guns, do you want to go?"

I smiled and said sure but then I got kind of angry because I was stuck in the truck with his cousin while he, Tony and Ian were on the back. It made me feel kind of like a two year old.

When we got to Wal-Mart I asked Billy

"Why did I get stuck in the front?"

"I want you safe that's why, and your mom would kill me if anything happened to you."

"I'm not two you know, and she would not, she trusts you."

He infuriated me but at the same time made me glad that he was looking after me. I walked with my hand in his through the store until we came to the hunting and guns section. Turns out he was looking for BB guns. I shook my head and thought, only boys and how did I get stuck in the middle of them?

After the boys bought the guns, we went back to Billy's and they started having a BB shooting war. I was just sitting there watching them and minding my own business when all of a sudden I felt a sting on my side. I looked around and found that Ian had shot me and next thing I knew Billy started shooting at me. I tried diving for a tree but Billy was slightly faster. He got me a few times then I hid behind a tree until it was over. After the match was over Billy came over to me, hugged me and kissed me.

Looking at the clock after a few minutes passed I realized it was time for me to go and Billy's cousin rode with us to take me home. I got in Angel's car and for once I got to ride in the front and it made me wonder if what I had said sunk in.

I went back to nanny's because momma was still there, and when I got out, I realized that Billy would be leaving in two days. We were all talking when Billy decided to take off his shirt and do a cannon ball into the pool. I smiled and said,

"You're crazy, but you are my kind of crazy."

When he got out he grabbed his shirt out of my hand and even though he was soaking wet gave me a big bear hug making me wet also. Billy told my mom and nanny goodbye and went to the car. I followed him and stood against the car door and kissed him softly and said

"I love you Billy and I will be here when you get back."

"I know you will Beka."

He got in the car and I kissed him again and waived bye because that would be the last time I saw him for two months.

Billy called me Monday because he was too busy to talk Sunday and he told me the he was about to leave for the airport and soon he would be heading to Fort Jackson South Carolina.

I told him that I loved him one last time and told him again that I would see him when he got back. The rest of the day was miserable for me but I knew that he would be back, I was just hoping that he wouldn't change too much.

Over the next couple of weeks I kept getting updates from his mom on the computer, and I slowly began to feel hurt because he had already called and written her twice, but I was glad that he was contacting someone. Then a week or two later Angel called me and gave me Billy's address so that I could write him, which made my heart leap with joy.

Later that evening I sat down and wrote Billy a long letter telling him about how much I missed him, what I had been up to, that I hoped he was doing well and that I couldn't wait to be back in his arms again.

I waited almost a week and got nothing, I started to believe that he wasn't going to write back. Then one day I didn't even check the mail and I had just got on the computer to listen to music when I heard:

"Beka, guess what? You have a letter from Billy."

I thought I was hearing things when my brother said it, but I was so happy that I didn't ask him to repeat himself instead I jumped with joy.

"Beka, do you want me to read it first?" my mom asked.

"No, mom I got it thanks." I yelled while opening the envelope.

I pulled out the letter and saw that his hand writing was really neat and I began to read:

Dear Beka,

I am happy to hear from you and I guess you got the address from my mom. I am doing well and it's really different down here. I have made a few new friends and I can't wait to see you and hold you in my arms again. I can say this I really miss you and love you a lot.

Love, Billy

I read that and had tears in my eyes because for the first time ever I felt that he really loved me. I let my mom read the letter and she thought it was sweet. After that I made sure I put the letter in a safe place so that I would never lose it.

The next few weeks I did my chores around the house and went swimming a few times. I wanted Billy home so bad but I could wait another month and a half I thought. Then one Sunday morning I got woke up at seven-thirty to my phone ringing. I leaned over and answered it before I could think and woke up to a huge surprise.

"Hey, baby what are you doing?" the voice said.

Once I realized it was Billy I snapped awake. Yawning I said,

"Nothing much just sleeping."

"Oh dang, sorry baby I didn't mean to wake you up, you need your sleep."

I smiled to myself and said,

"That's alright darling."

We talked for a couple more minutes about how my summer was going and how basic was going then sadly he had to go. I knew I would miss him more after talking to him, but I also knew I would live now that I knew he missed and loved me for sure.

    After the phone call I got up and got on my computer, I was too awake to go back to sleep. I got on my Myspace and looked at the pictures of Billy and me and thought that we were the most perfect couple. I clicked on Billy's profile because I noticed it said that he had been online. I scrolled down and my heart sunk because I saw a comment that I didn't want to believe. It was from a girl named

Courtney saying that she enjoyed hanging with him right before he left and that they needed to do it again. I knew what I was reading but I didn't want to believe it. I waited on my mom to get up and when she did I told her that Billy had called me.

"That's good baby, so is everything alright?"

"Yes, Mom, why wouldn't it be?" I asked

"I just don't want you to get hurt. He could come back and change his mind you know."

"Oh no, please, Mom, do not say that and I hope he doesn't."

But truthfully that was what I was worried the most about.

I was in the living room the following Tuesday when my brother came in and told me that I had another letter. I smiled in happiness and basically ripped it open, but when I opened this one I was in shock because this later was longer than the other. This letter was two and a half pages.

The letter talked about how he had surprised me with the phone call the other day and how he had got smoked by one of the army sergeants. Then the letter stated about how he didn't have much more time to go over there and that he couldn't wait to get back to family, me, friends and the best take out dinner ever Chinese. That statement made me smile.

Over the next few weeks I noticed how August 28th was only six more weeks away and that in six weeks I would be back in my soldier's arms. It was Friday night and I had a party to go to the next day. It was formal so I had a hard time deciding on what to wear.

Saturday evening after I tried on a bunch of dresses we came to the decision that I would wear a black party dress that my mom had in her closet that fit me. I slid the dress on, looked in the mirror and smiled because I liked how the dress fit on me. It was black with thin straps and the length came down to my knees.

When I finished getting ready I went to the party expecting to have fun. It was my friends sixteenth birthday and she was having her party at the Radisson Hotel which was a really fancy place.

When I got there I found that Leigh was already there which made me happy. I then found out that our friend Shea was coming, but she was going to be late as usual. When Shea finally arrived she arrived with her boyfriend and her sister's boyfriend.

The party was going great and the food was amazing, but then it came down to dancing and I was ready. Shea and I got up on the dance floor and had a great time until her sister's boyfriend decided to slap my butt. I told Shea in the bathroom what happened and she went up to him and slapped him in the face. I tried not to laugh but it was funny. The party was great but after it was over my feet hurt so bad.

After I got home I put on my Pajamas and went straight to bed because I was wore out. I was sleeping so well when my phone rang at eight-thirty. I looked over and saw that it was restricted like it had been last weekend. I answered it to find that it was Billy again and I was very excited.

He told me that he missed me and that he loved me and a little about his week. I told him about the party and about the guy slapping my butt and about Shea punching him in the face which he thought was funny. Then after that we talked for a few more minutes before he had to go. After getting off the phone with him that time I realized that he only had two more weeks to go.

The two weeks went by fast to my advantage, and the Sunday morning before the first day of school and a week until I would be back in his arms, I stayed the night at my cousins house and woke up to my phone ringing the next morning.

"Hello." I said softly.

"Hey, baby, what are you doing?" Billy asked.

"Sleeping and I'm going to shoot you for waking me up." I said jokingly.

"Well, fine. I can always hang up and call Ian if you want."

"Please don't, you know I love hearing from you baby."

We talked for a little bit then we hung up because he was on a time limit. As I hung up I thought to myself "only a few more days".

Sophomore Year!

I went to school excited the next morning for two reasons: One It was sophomore year and two Billy would be home in only two days. The excitement got cut short fast though because when I walked out into the Eagle Court that morning Marie was already out there running her mouth.

She was running her mouth about how Billy had been cheating on me before he left and about how he was going to break up with me when he got back. I was tired of hearing it so I was determined to put an end to it.

"Hey, damn you, Marie, Billy and I are staying together so shut your mouth or I am going to shut it for you."

I said to her and I meant it to. This girl could only take so much.

The rest of my day went fairly well. I found out that I had Geometry,

Agriscience, Civics and Film Critique. I learned that I had Film with Meredith and Billy since he had to come back to get three more credits. Film was also with Mrs. Janice so that was another plus and the class wasn't hard at all. The objective was to watch movies and write about them and every other week write a movie report. That was the best class a school could have.

The next few days went along good. It was Friday and I knew Billy would be coming home today. I was sitting in third period when my friend Roper came up to me and said,

"Billy was just in the guidance office getting his schedule."

My heart was pounding and I replied back,

"Why didn't you come get me sooner? I should go postal on you, Roper!"

By Postal I meant beat him up.

I asked to go to the bath room and rushed by the guidance office but he wasn't there he had already left. I sighed and went back to class. After fourth as I was getting on the bus I received a picture from Billy in his uniform and it about made me cry. I responded back telling him how proud of him I was and that he was now my soldier.

When I got home I called him and I got to talk to him for a few minutes. He said he was tired but he was happy to be home and that he would call me later. I was happy to hear the words "I love you" again when he said them, but little did I know that was going to be the last time I heard those words.

The next morning I texted him and asked him what he was up to and if I would get to see him before Monday. When he responded it shook my world because he exploded on me saying that he was trying to spend time with his family and that I made it sound as if I didn't want him too. Him saying that made me extremely confused and hurt at the same time. I took the phone to my mom and she called him to see what was wrong because she couldn't stand to see me cry. After she was finished she told me not to call him unless he called me and so I didn't.

    I woke up the next morning crying and I couldn't figure out why and my chest ached like there was a hole in it. I got up and did my morning routine. I then spent my day outside listening to my iPod. I was outside listening to "Baby Don't Go" By Fabulous when I received a text message from Billy. I opened it and it read,

"I think it is best that we break up."

I read that and found myself sobbing. I was ripped apart because he left and confused because he gave no explanation to why he left and still to this day I still don't know the truth.

 I tried to figure out how he could say he loved me one day then the next just end it like that. That whole day mom tried cheering me up but couldn't. What hurt the most is that I had wasted my whole summer waiting on him and staying faithful for nothing. That night I ended up crying myself to sleep.

 The next morning was horrible, everyone including Marie was rubbing it in my face that he had left me. I quickly found myself sobbing in a bathroom stall until the bell rang for first period and even then I was still crying in that class. Which I had warned Mrs. Lorna when I had arrived to class that I was having a bad day.

After first period I was out in the Eagle Court and the moment that I had been waiting for all morning came. The doors opened and Billy came prancing out into the Eagle Court smiling ear to ear. We locked eyes and I felt my heart breaking all over again. I felt a tear drop and dried it up quick and walked over to him and asked to speak with him a minute. I noticed that everyone was watching us and I asked him why he had left me all of a sudden. His answer to me was,

"My mom doesn't want us together, and if you don't believe me, then ask her. And I want to be single for right now."

I thought hogwash and I ran to second period crying again after I yelled "Bullshit".

The rest of my day got worse but at least that semester I didn't have lunch with him. By the time fourth period rolled around I was crying so bad that I couldn't stop. Meredith gave me a hug before she walked in, told Mrs. Janice that I was having a bad day and sat down behind me.

When Billy came in the class was half empty but Billy being the person he was sat down right across from me. I simply buried my head into my jacket so he couldn't see the tears and sobbed quietly. I was wiping a tear when I heard him lean over and ask Meredith,

"What is wrong with her?"

She responded with,

"Are you seriously asking me that?"

I felt like punching him in the face.

When the bell rung for class to end I couldn't have been happier. Only when the announcements came on did I lift my head up and only then did Billy see how upset I was. We locked eyes again as I was leaving.

When I got home I curled up on my bed trying to forget about him only to find myself reading the letters he wrote. I was tired of the pain and I just wanted it and everything in my life to go away. I then remembered what Billy had said and I knew he believed I would never ask her so I decided to email Angel and tell her what Billy had said.

Later that evening Angel called me.

"Hey, I got your message, what's going exactly going on?" Angel asked.

"Angel, Billy said that he broke up with me because you made him. He said that you didn't want us together."

"Beka, that's not true, All I told him was that if he didn't love you then he needed to be fair to you, and that he needed to follow his heart."

After hearing her confirm that what I thought was right I was confused even more and I realized that Billy had lied to me. Why? The next thing I heard was Billy walking through the door and Angel yelling

"YOU'RE RIDING WITH ME TO GET YOUR BROTHER NOW! GET IN THE CAR!"

I heard that and thought he's in trouble.

The next day at school was a little bit better. It was more anger than hurt. Classes went a little smoother and

Mrs. Kim was even glad that I was in a better mood. Shea made my day better by drawing me a picture of a woman being unchained from a broken heart. She was quite an artist back in high school.

When fourth period rolled around that day Billy decided he would sit behind me and torture me some more. This time though I was forced to stay awake and watch the movie because there was a paper to be filled out about different camera angles and shots found throughout the movie. As I was watching the movie it was torture because I could feel every breath Billy took go down my neck. Then I felt him touch my back and I shut eyes fighting back tears.

After the movie we still had some time before class was over I put my head down. Then all of a sudden I felt a finger go down the side of my ear on my hot spot. My head shot straight up as an automatic response and I had tears in my eyes. He was standing there beside me and Mrs. Janice had gone out of the room.

"Why are you doing this to me?" I asked

"Look I'm sorry okay, and I still want us to be friends."

"Screw you Billy." I said. I waited on you for two months, stayed faithful, and got letters from you telling me that you loved me only to get dumped when you got back. No screw you."

By then Mrs. Janice had walked back in how much she had heard I'm not sure because she never said anything.

Homecoming came around and Billy was still trying to talk to me and act like nothing had ever happened. It was like he couldn't see how bad he had hurt me. Homecoming was a day where we had pep rallies and events and had no class work.

Well so happens this homecoming after the pep rally and the parade that the school has every year on the football field the FFA club was sponsoring Karaoke. I decided that I was going to do it. I decided to dedicate a song to Billy. I sung another Dixie Chicks song. I sung Traveling Soldier and made eye contact with him the whole time.

Over the next few months his stories kept changing to why he left and I had gave up hope to ever knowing the truth to why he left me. We had some what made peace especially after I threw the letters he wrote me in his face one morning and because I had come to the conclusion later on that I would rather have him in my life as a friend then not at all.

On my sixteenth birthday I skipped school and spent the day with nanny. She made me a Conway Twitty CD because I absolutely love his music. When school ended Billy called me and told me happy birthday. That had made my day even though momma and nanny had not forgiven him yet for hurting me. I knew it was over between us but deep down I didn't want it to be.

It was close to the end of the semester and I had to stay after for my Civics review. Before I had to be in class, Meredith, Billy and I were talking in the hallway when Meredith had to go catch up with her sister. Billy got to close to me and it sent urges throughout my body.

"You might not want to do that." I warned.

"If you are going to kiss me don't do it here."

I looked at him confusingly and before I realized it we were outside and I was standing against a concrete wall. Our lips touched for the first time in months and it was like I was in heaven again. After he pulled away I asked him again why he left and his excuse this time was my age and my maturity level.

    I did really well at the review session, but I couldn't get my mind off Billy and the kiss. When my mom picked me up I told her about what had happened and she was as confused as I was and we couldn't put our finger on it.

    The next day I was worried about my math exam because I am horrible when it comes to math and I was afraid I was not going to pass and I didn't pass but that was okay I'd tried. The next day's exam was better it was Agriscience and I made an 80 on it.

After the exam was over, I had just gotten my lunch when Billy said

"If you want me to take you home, you better come on."

It took me only a second to think and I was in the front seat with Billy again, which made me more and more confused but happy at the same time. He took me home the rest of my exam days and each day he kissed me like we were still together. I was so confused that I couldn't think.

The new semester started which was good for me the only thing that sucked was Billy was finally done with high school. He did still call me though and Meredith had moved but luckily she moved right up the road from me so I still got to hang out with her. She had to switch schools though because of the district change.

My classes spring semester was English 2 honors, Horticulture, Biology and Chorus 2. It was an okay schedule. Fourth period was good and bad because I had it with Leigh, Cassie, and my friend Brina. The bad part was Katie was in there also.

As the semester passed Billy and I still talked on the phone. Then one Thursday night in March after he got through with PT he swung by my house, he had looked so sexy in his uniform it made me smile. I loved seeing him in it. He had brought by a plate of fish that he had prepared himself because there was extras left over. Turns out his job in the reserves was to be the cook. When I walked him out he gave me a big hug and kiss and left. The fish was great but that didn't help the confusion.

A couple months later, on a Friday night Billy asked to come over to my house which really surprised me. Then it hit me he was coming over because his mom was at the George Strait and Reba concert. When he got to my house Momma and her friend from up the street were trying to put up a dart board in her room when it broke. It was not long after that until Billy and I had the house to ourselves, and I went over to put on a pot of tea. Billy then said

"You can put that on or you can come over here and make out with me."

I slowly sat the tea pot down and went over to him and softly kissed him. Then he picked me up and laid me down on the couch. I thought of how right it felt. I laid there with my arms around his neck kissing him for a few minutes. Then I got up and put the tea on. I turned around to find that Billy had the fly swat in his hands and was swatting me with it playfully.

I smiled at him then he threw it down and laughed and gently wrapped his arms around me and held me like he used to which fluttered my heart and made me happy again.

We stayed like that for a few minutes until he had to leave. He had to get home before his mom got home. After he left I felt the pain all over again because something told me that he wouldn't be coming back.

Monday school was great but I still had Billy on my mind, and I kept asking myself "Are we getting back together?" because I was really getting tired of the mind tricks. As fourth period rolled around I noticed Katie staring at me and it was starting to aggravate me. As Brina came in I went over to her and sat next to her who sat next to Katie sadly.

"Beka, do you want to know what I really hate?"

"What Brina?" I asked

"Guys that are cheaters?"

"I'm not sure if all guys are like that but I do know that I want a guy that is really sweet and that I can see every day or once or twice a week." I responded with.

"Yeah me too but where are they?"

Brina said before class started. Our conversations were very random sometimes.

I went home that afternoon singing a song from class that day when my phone rung. I had just gotten it on the charger too. It was Billy I was in a good mood so I said

"Hello" in a cheerful voice.

"Hey can you tell me what the hell is going on." He said frazzled.

"What are you talking about?" I asked clueless.

"Someone who wouldn't lie to me told me that you have been going around saying that I come to your house every day or at least once or twice a week."

"WHAT! Billy I swear I never said such a thing."

"Well, this person would never lie to me."

"So you're saying I am? I have never lied to you before so why would I start now?"

"Look I don't believe you, so lose my number and never call me again."

He said then hung up. I was so dumbfounded and the pain came again. I never said anything to him but I automatically knew who said it.

 I went to fourth period the next day hurt and very angry, but I kept my mouth shut because I was at school. I knew deep down Billy was with Katie now, but why did she lie on me? I never did anything to her. I sat down next to Brina and told her about what had happened and made sure Katie knew I was mad but it didn't seem to faze her. She had gotten what she had wanted and she didn't care how she had gotten it.

 A month later, my uncle Ray passed away and Billy had added me back on Myspace. I got on, on my cousins computer the day before the funeral and found a message from him saying,

"I added you but I will not tolerate any flirting from you, I have got a girlfriend now so don't even talk about us getting back together or I will delete you and never talk to you again".

I thought, wow delete me, that's so bad. I was already in a bad mood and the crap from him made it worse. So I wrote back:

"Look, I don't care whether you have a girlfriend or not and why would I flirt with an ass wipe like you?"

After he read that message he blocked me but I didn't care.

In May, I went to my FFA meeting. I had started FFA in the fall that year but we didn't get to do that much because Mrs. Kim was a very busy but outstanding teacher. Katie had to be there sadly because she was an officer. I didn't say a word to her, but I heard her friend Tonie tell one of the guys that she was with Billy.

"Tonie shut up." Katie said.

"Oh you're fine. I don't see why you hide it from her anyway. She already knows."

I thought to myself "Oh so I was right".

 A couple weeks later we had our first chorus concert and Billy came which shocked me. Katie had a solo which I'm not going to lie I was jealous over because I don't recall how many times I had tried out for a solo and had never gotten one.

 After the concert I quickly found momma, nanny and my brother because seeing Billy and Katie together just tore me apart more and more. When I got in the car I was told that he kept eye balling me and that he wouldn't even speak to my mom or nanny. Had he really become that big of a prick I wondered?

Over that summer Billy had gone to AIT training, the training after basic, and I found myself texting him asking him how he was at random moments and I didn't even know why.

One weekend I stayed the night with Meredith and Billy called her. I sat there quietly but when she told him I was there he quickly had to go. I asked her,

"What is his problem with me? I haven't done anything."

She looked at me and responded,

"Beka I'm not sure and he usually tells me everything you know that."

Throughout that summer I kept asking myself and even Meredith wasn't even exactly sure why Billy hated me so much, or even what I had done that was so wrong? It was a Saturday in July and I decided I would text Billy. I texted him and asked him how he was doing but the response I got wasn't from him. It was from Katie and it wasn't a very nice one.

"You Bitch, leave him alone and if you don't I am going to find out where you live and come kick your ass."

I laughed because I thought she was funny seeing as how she was shorter than I was and I'm only five foot one. So I responded with

"Bring it on, Katie, I ain't scared."

That started it. The next thing I knew her friend was calling me. At first I simply hung up on her then I thought about it and thought how immature of me that was and called her back and talked to her. After talking with her she understood why I was trying to talk with Billy and for a little bit things were peaceful.

After the conversation with Katie's friend I had decided to put on my pajamas and fix my DVD player because for some reason it was having issues with my television. I had just gotten content with it when I heard a knock at the front door.

"Who are you?" I heard John my mom's friend say.

I then heard Billy's voice, and I dropped the screwdriver and flew out of my bedroom in rage.

"Oh no, you aren't coming in here." My mom said while getting in between us.

"Its fine mom, I will talk but only if he's alone." I said while looking at Billy.

It wasn't pretty when we got outside because mom again stood in between us so I couldn't smack him in the face like I wanted to. Billy then rambled on about how he told me never to call him again and that it was over and I interrupted,

"Look, the only reason I have been texting you is because I want to know what I did that was so wrong to make you hate me so much. First you come to my house, make out with me, and then call me the next day and say, "I never want to speak to you again." So you darn right I am mad." I said not so calmly.

After that he didn't have anything to say. He didn't like seeing that side of me.

Then my mom butted in

"Beka, I know this hurts you, and I know what I'm about to say is going to only hurt worse but face it baby girl, he only wanted one thing." my mom said to me.

Then turning to Billy she said.

"Isn't that right Mr. Billy?"

"That wasn't it at all, I swear."

"Then what was it?"

There was no response so my mom nodded and continued and all along I stood there fighting back tears.

"Well Billy since you had the guts to come here I'm going to make this all better. Beka don't call him, don't text him and if you see him don't even look at him."

She then asked Billy if he was happy now and he was.

"Beka, I'm sorry that it had to come to this. I really am."

I felt more broken now because he still had not spoken the truth that I still wanted to know, but then as I was turning away I got another slap in the face with the words

"I don't love you anymore".

I quickly turned away so he couldn't see my pain and I again ended up crying myself to sleep that night.

    The rest of the summer I spent trying to forget about Billy and about the love we shared and about the good times. I still went to Meredith's house a lot and we would hang out and have a blast and I would forget all about the pain. Until Billy would call or text her, then the pain would come right back. All that time I hadn't even thought about seeing anyone else because I didn't think it would be fair to that person since I knew I was in love with someone else.

Then one night a few weeks before school started back my sister set me up on a blind date with another guy from the military. She said he was really sweet but the date went horrible. He hardly talked at all and later on he turned out to be a real douche bag. The date went so bad that I don't even remember his name.

I went to my sister's house a couple of weeks later and told her thanks but no thanks about the worse blind date ever. She was shocked she thought he would have been great for me. She was as mad at Billy as everyone else for putting me through hell and back.

I had a good time at her house like always because I was able to get away from all the stress, away from

Thomasville and away from Billy and the drama. There at my sisters I stayed up late and talked to her about everything and how I felt. I even played with my little niece whom I love so very, very much. But everything has to go back to reality. I went back to Thomasville a week later because junior year, my worst year was approaching.

Junior Year!

Junior year started out great. I was determined to forget all about Billy and to push him out of my mind completely and to try and move on. It was a new year and I wanted a fresh start. I even decided that I would forget all about Katie. Like Shae told me before if she wanted sloppy seconds then she could have him. I now agreed. I walked out into the Eagle Court that morning with a clear conscious.

Seeing all my friends made me ecstatic after a horrible summer. Well most of my friends because Cassie had switched to extended day. I did meet some new friends. John and Lisa. Lisa was really cool she was a freshman and we had a lot in common like the types of books we liked to read. I also met up with Leigh that morning before homeroom and told her what happened over the summer and she couldn't believe it. "Girl you just need to forget about him and move on. I am telling you because you can do so much better."

She said as the bell rung.

First period was interesting because I had US History with Mr. Kevin and he was crazy. Well more like insane but he made class really fun in ways that made people want to learn. Kevin was also young probably in his mid-thirties so he could relate with all his students. Also I knew I was going to enjoy his class because one I love history and two I had his class with Leigh and Lyndsay.

After first period I went to yearbook class which really interested me because I was going to get to see how the yearbook was made and I was actually going to be a part of making it. The first day went well, we went over all the basics and were assigned what pages we would be doing. I was assigned the academic pages with a guy named James and the quick reads with a girl named Jamie.

Third period was Horticulture one, It was one of Mrs. Kim's classes so I knew I was going to like it. We did our normal routine which was a journal at the beginning of class then notes. This time though the notes were about plants and flowers. The only thing I didn't like about the class was Plant ID which is where you learn the characteristics of a plant then you have to identify it by the characteristics while looking at a picture. She would assign us plants on Monday and we would have a quiz every Friday. It sounded easy but it wasn't.

Fourth period was one of my favorites also because it was Music

Appreciation and Journalism. I was juggling two classes at once. Challenging yes, but I loved it. I got to listen to music and rate it on whether I liked it or not. So far I loved that year and I loved my classes because while I stayed busy I had no time to think about Billy.

 I went home after school and realized that I had actually had a good day. I did my homework and when mom got home I told her about how my day went. She was glad that I had a good day and later that night I texted Meredith to see how her first day had gone. Surprisingly hers had gone great as well. We talked for a while that night then I went to bed hoping for another great day the next day.

 The next day was even better. We got started right away in yearbook which I really enjoyed because I basically got to stay out of class the whole period every day to take pictures of people. I would occasionally help my partner with the pages but ninety-eight percent of the time I was the one out taking pictures. It was great and really fun.

I had an excellent week and on that Friday Mrs. Kim announced that Monday she would be having a meeting for the people interested in being an FFA officer. She explained that the ones that stayed after would be interviewed one on one with her about the position they wanted to run for. She made the announcement in all her classes and I got excited because I knew that I had what it took to be an officer. I just couldn't decide which position I wanted to run for.

That Monday morning I was all excited about staying after for my interview and I had decided that I would run for FFA Reporter. When I arrived to first period my good mood quickly got shot down because Mr. Kevin announced that in October which was a month away that he would be leaving for a position at Ledford. The whole class was upset because we all enjoyed having him as a teacher. We knew he would be missed by many.

After that the rest of the day went by okay, not as good as normal but okay. I guess it was because of the news in first period and then failing a quiz in journalism. When it was time for my meeting I quickly forgot about my bad day and got excited and nervous at the same time.

When I arrived to Mrs. Kim's room there were already some people in there and one of the people was

Tonie. Before the interviews started she told all of us that she was going to interview us one on one and that her decision would be posted on her door tomorrow morning and that after we were done we could leave. I waited patiently for my turn I was one of the last ones to be interviewed since I was running for reporter. When I was done I was so afraid that I had blew it because I had been extremely nervous.

When I got home I chilled the rest of the night and hoped that I had gotten the position in FFA because I was really sure that I had what it took to be an officer. I talked to Meredith a few minutes that night then I got ready for bed hoping that I would bring home good news the next day.

The next morning I got up more than ready to get to school. Mom wished me good luck and I went to catch the bus. When I arrived to school I hung out in the Eagle Court like normal and I was talking with Leigh when Katie decided to walk out. She watched me like a hawk and gave me go to hell looks and it took all I had not to punch her in the face. So me being me I just smiled at her and gave her the finger on both hands. She didn't like that too much.

    Seeing Katie didn't start my day off good but I wasn't going to let her ruin it. I was sitting in first period doing a note packet when all of a sudden a man not too much older with a very sexy ass (and when I mean sexy, I mean it was the kind of ass where you just wanted to grab it and shake it) walked in. He was very handsome as well but his looks had nothing on that ass. As he walked all the way in all the girls heads popped up, Lyndsay and I exchanged looks and I heard our friend Kim say,

"Damn that's fine".

It then hit me and I responded to both of them

"How much do y'all want to bet that he is going to be our new teacher?"

Sure enough I was right. The guy with the sexy ass was Mr. Thomas who would be starting that week after homecoming.

After first I went to yearbook and for once I was ready to get it over with because I was ready to see the results. I went in for a quick meeting about the senior pages then went and started my normal task of taking pictures. After a time though to be honest it got a little boring. Finally once eleven-thirty rolled around I quickly rushed to Horticulture. When I got there my heart sunk for a few seconds because I didn't get reporter, but once I saw that I got the position of Sentinel I quickly became excited again.

I went into class said good morning to Zoodle (the class Guinea pig) sat dawn and began to do my journal. Class was interesting that day because we were learning about how a plants reproductive system worked.

I was sitting in my seat taking notes and waiting on the bell to ring for lunch when I got called to the guidance office. I put my pencil down and looked up confusingly and started racking my brain trying to figure out why I was being called because Marie had graduated so I couldn't think of another reason to why I was being called.

When I got to the guidance office I found out that it was because of

Katie. She had come to the guidance office telling them that I had threatened her which I didn't but of course she had already taken Katie's side. I was told that if I was called back up there that I would be suspended. My thought was "what the hell" I went to lunch pissed but I tried to have a good rest of the day.

Fourth period was the best that day. We were doing a chapter on country music in Music Appreciation so I got to do a project on Conway Twitty and listen to some old country. Also in journalism I got to do an editorial on cellphones. I was busy that class period and it took my mind off Katie and I enjoyed what I was doing.

A week later was homecoming for Meredith and that Friday night I stayed with her and went to her school's homecoming game with her. I walked into South Davidson High School for the first time ever and thought wow because it was ten times bigger than East. I met a few of her friends and then we went out and watched the game. I missed seeing her all the time but she seemed to like South better and I could tell why.

We were having a blast at the game watching the players, laughing, eating snacks when Billy decided to call. When she answered it hit me all over again the pain and I couldn't breathe. She told him that she was at the game with me and he quickly had to go. She apologized but I told her that it wasn't her fault. I didn't let him ruin my night. We watched the half time show, the rest of the game and went back to her house where I learned to play guitar hero.

A week later was homecoming for East and like always the week was crazy. It was also bittersweet because Friday was Kevin's last day and the week sadly went by way to fast. On Thursday at the end of class Kevin told us how he enjoyed getting to know each and every one of us and that we would all truly be missed. He left that Friday but he didn't stay gone long he came back at the beginning of the 2012/2013 school year.

On Friday like normal we had the pep rallies and the parade outside and the afternoon activities. I did karaoke again but this time to Listen to Your Heart by DHT and I did horrible because I was sick at the time. That night was the game and Meredith went with me since I had went with her to the South game.

The game started out great I introduced her to some of my new friends and we were having a good time laughing and cutting up. That was until halftime and Billy had started texting. She told him that she was at the game with me and his response was,

"Why are you at the game with her? You don't go to that school anymore?"

I knew he would have something to say but I didn't care. As she was texting him I was having one of my immature moments by giving her phone the finger every time he would send a text. My friend Rhiannon who was chilling with us thought it was funny.

"Beka do you really have to do that?"

"Meredith it's not for you, it's for him and if he was here I would do it to his face." I said

"You know he wouldn't show, and he is with Katie right now."

"Screw Katie, and I dare you to send him a picture of me giving the finger." I said smiling. "You know I can't do that, Billy would never talk to me again."

"I'll do it." Rhiannon said while jumping off the bleachers.

After she took the picture and sent it to him I started laughing because like I said that was one of my immature moments.

It was not long after that that he started blowing up Meredith's phone.

"Say some random girl took your phone and that she took the picture of

Beka gigging her boyfriend but sent it to him by accident." Rhiannon said.

It sounded like a reasonable excuse but would Billy be dumb enough to buy it was the question. She told him and he stopped being angry with her but it was not fifth teen minutes later when I received a phone call from my mom saying that she was on her way and that I was in big trouble. I asked her why and turned out Billy had went to my house and showed her the picture. He didn't believe the story but I couldn't believe that he had actually went and tattled on me.

    When my mom got there I told her the story that Rhiannon came up with and thankfully she did believe it. After that night though Meredith and I stopped hanging out a lot because Billy made her choose who she wanted to be friends with. According to him she couldn't be friends with us both which left me feeling confused and betrayed again.

Monday started a new day and as I went to first period I knew that it was going to be an interesting day. I was the first one in the class and after I sat down that morning I started to read Catching Fire from the Hunger Games series. I thought it was really interesting. I was at the part where Peeta had just been kidnapped. I was getting in to it when our new teacher walked in and started writing something on the board.

I was mesmerized because I'm not going to lie that man was handsome. He was not tall but not too short either, with a little muscle and brown eyes and the kind of facial hair that if you cut it you would just not look right as a man. I had went to my own little world when Lyndsay came in, she rolled her eyes at me.

"Beka, earth to Beka." She said while waving her hand in my face.

"What?"

"Pay attention girl, so how was your weekend?"

"It was okay I guess." Then the final bell rung and it was time to start the day.

    The first thirty minutes of class we got an introduction from our new teacher about himself. His name was Mr. Thomas and he had graduated from East in 04. We learned a lot about him and he seemed like he would be a cool teacher but something told me that he would never be Mr. Kevin. I knew I would give him a chance and I hoped the rest of the class would too. After he introduced himself we continued with the lesson we had started Thursday.

Months went by and he had actually been teaching the class really well. I had started to forget all about Billy and I got more mature. As the semester ended and half of the next semester rolled around Prom became the subject of the school. At the end of March I went and stayed the night with Brina and we had a blast and then she started talking about this guy that she had been talking to and was interested in.

"So what is his name?" I asked curiously.

"Frankie Hewitt, he goes to Thomasville."

Hearing that I about spit out the water I was drinking because I knew exactly who she was talking about.

Frankie and I had dated in eighth grade and we really cared about each other but it ended up being complicated because his dad wanted him to focus more on his studies then girls. As I told her that I knew him and that the rumor was that he was a player she called him.

She asked him if what I had told her was true and he didn't deny it. He asked if he could come over and hang with the both of us since he hadn't seen me in forever. He gave me his number and told him to text him later because mom had come to pick me up before he could arrive.

I began texting him later that night and we played catch up for a little while. He told me that he had changed and that he no longer lived with his dad and that he still cared about me. We talked for a while and then we decided to web cam together on the computer. After seeing him I noticed that nothing had really changed when it came to his features except for his muscles. He had developed those quite well.

We talked every day after that and he asked if I would like for him to be my prom date and I assured him that I would love it if he would take me to prom. We continued to talk every day and even got back together on April 2nd.

Frankie and I would hang out on the days that he had off from work because he work night shifts at Walmart in High Point. I did think he was a little crazy though because he insisted on driving a blue VIP moped which scared the shit out of me.

Our relationship was one of the best that I had ever been in. He would call me and leave me sweet messages during the day before he went to bed. Then at night on his break he would send me a text message so I would find it when I woke up the next morning.

The times that he would come over would be the best and I fell deeply in love with him and thought no more of Billy. The week before Easter he came over before work to sign the guest paper for prom. After he signed it he stayed for a few minutes with me sitting on his lap wrapped in his arms. He kissed me and told me how much I meant to him and that he never wanted to loose me again. I felt like I had actually found my one.

A week went by and school let out for Easter Break. I was excited because I have always loved the holiday of Easter. Not because of the so called Easter Bunny or candy but because of the true meaning. That Saturday the day before Easter, Frankie came by to hang out with me and my cousin Michelle who was staying the night with me. We three chatted and then Frankie decided to tickle me all over and on my feet to where I couldn't move. I ended up rolling of the couch laughing.

 He left shortly after he got a call from a friend asking for assistance for something around eight o'clock. I walked outside with him and he politely kissed and then bit my lip hard. I smiled at him and kissed him again and told him to be careful. He told me he loved me and left.

 An hour later he called me and I told him about a dream that I had had of us getting married under the pecan tree at nanny's.

"Beka baby don't say that because you never know what the future has in store for us."

"I know but Frankie I do love you and I don't want anything to ever happen to us again."

"I know you don't I don't either but promise me that if anything ever happens to me that you won't dwell and that you will move on and live your life. Promise me."

I promised him but when he said those words I got a little worried because I didn't know what I would do if anything ever happened to him.

Still to this day I hear those words and I still taste the last kissed we shared. I say this because that April 24th 2011, Easter Sunday Frankie Laverne Hewitt JR. The one that I had fallen in love with all over again got killed on his moped in a car accident a couple hours later after his last phone call to me.

"Hey baby, what color is your prom dress again? Okay baby I got to go I love you."

I truly believe that he really did know otherwise he wouldn't have made the remark he did the night before.

The Funeral a few days later on the 28th was the hardest thing I think I have ever had to do. Seeing the one that showed me that it was okay to love again being put into the ground tore me apart. I didn't know how I was going to deal with it.

I still went to prom because I know that he would have wanted me to. I went with my good friend Lawerence who I had been friends with since my freshman year. I wore a Lilac purple dress and managed to have a good time even though it was hard.

That June when school let out I went over to Meredith's one Friday night. I was still hurting really bad but it was slowly getting easier. On Saturday Meredith got a phone call from Billy. He knew what I had been going through.

Billy came over to Meredith's later that day with me there. Once I saw him and how much he'd changed I started falling for him all over again. He said it was because I was obsessed with him but it wasn't. If there was one thing that Frankie taught me it was that true love never dies.

We all three hung out like old times even though there was some tension in the room and when Meredith had snuck off to the bathroom Billy got close to me and bit my neck. It sent urges throughout my entire body and the next thing I knew I was on his lap with him kissing me.

I didn't know what to think but I guess since losing Frankie I would take anyone that would let me lean on them. It didn't end there for Billy and I, he started coming over to my house to hang out and I would go over to his to have whenever booty calls and to be with him whenever he wanted. I was being used again but I didn't care I just wanted to forget about the pain of losing Frankie.

Billy being back didn't last long however. When August rolled around Billy left again assuring me that this time it was for good and I was determined to be done with him. I felt that I deserved better and that I could find better again sometime.

SENIOR YEAR!

Senior year started with a bang, I was sure to have a drama free year. I had gotten with a guy named Stone whose family had known mine all their lives. He was great and he seemed like he really cared for me.

We did a lot of things together when he wasn't grounded and momma liked him. The only bad thing was that he went to Extended Day but he did live about a mile up the road from me.

Senior Year was great compared to all of the rest. First semester I had English 4 honors with Mrs. Jill who was awesome, Earth and Environmental resources 1 with Mrs. Kim, Tech Math 2 with Mr. Danny and Psychology with the one and only Coach T. I loved all my teachers that semester and I made WONDERFUL grades.

The next semester was great too I only had three class periods and I got to leave. It was the best semester that I had ever had at East. I took French 2 that semester and learned a lot. I even stayed in the library whenever I wasn't in class. By the time I graduated I had friends not teachers.

Billy came back into my life in April 2012 after my eighteenth birthday. It got to the point that I was hardly seeing Stone anymore. The romantic things started with Billy and I again. I would go over and to hang out with him during the week after he got home from work and it would always result into us making love and cuddling with one another.

We kept getting closer and closer again and this time I was determined for it to be the last shot. Prom that year was really interesting because Leigh and I went together. She wore a midnight blue dress and I wore a red dress. I looked absolutely gorgeous on me.

Billy started texting me way before we even got to prom. He was half drunk and that was when I could always get the truth out of him. Leigh and I got to prom and automatically got bored. It was nothing like it was Junior Year. Leigh and I got so bored that we ended up leaving an hour after prom started.

We left and went to Billy's where things ended up getting crazy. He was past drunk when we got there but it was still hilarious. By that I mean when we got there he decided to kiss me, then lead me to his bedroom where we had a quick make out session and then he picked me up, laid me on his shoulders and carried me through the garage like a sack of taters. He about hit my head on the garage door but luckily I it by a couple inched.

He then decided to dry hump Leigh's car before passing out in the drive way. The boring night turned crazy. Leigh and I couldn't get him to wake up so we ended up leaving with him still passed out in the driveway.

He didn't remember anything the next morning but when I told him he couldn't believe his actions. He hung up with me and called Leigh to apologize.

We officially got back together in July that year after graduation I thought it would be perfect but it wasn't he decided he had to have me and Meredith at the same time. When he wasn't with one he was with the other. It hurt that he was doing it but I loved Billy and I wanted him no matter what the cost. This lasted a couple weeks and then he ended it with the excuse why be someone that you know you could never love? It broke me into pieces again at first but I later found out that it was for the best. That I didn't need him or Meredith in my life to be happy.

COLLEGE LIFE!

I started college at GTCC in August that year and I had the best time in all my life. People always told me that college was way harder than High School but to me it was much easier. I made straight A's and B's that semester with a GPA of 3.4. I had awesome instructors that really enjoyed helping their students if they needed it. I won't lie it its hard work but it is worth it.

I met who is now my husband in September of that year and we have been together ever since. We ended up getting pregnant in October that year and we got married in April of 2013. Our daughter Lena Marie was born in July of 2013 so I now have a husband, a wonderful daughter and an amazing step-daughter who I look at as my own.

People has always said fight for love and they are right to an extent. You fight for love until it reaches a certain point. I could have continued to fight for Billy but if I had I wouldn't have the family that I have now with a great mother in-law who yes occasionally drives me bonkers and a grandmother in-law who drives me bonkers all the time but I still love her.

I am still currently in college because I had to take two semesters off after getting pregnant with Lena due to complications but I am working on my physical therapy degree as well as my dream of being an author. This is my second book. If you like mystery, fantasy and romance look up my first book The Everlasting Love: The Beginning.

The moral that I am trying to get across in this book if you haven't gotten it already is to Never be afraid to love and love again but don't take any shit either because there is always something better waiting for you. You just have to search for it.

Made in the USA
Middletown, DE
05 February 2023

23239124R00085